# AGENT MOOSE
## MOOSE ON A MISSION

WITH ART BY

**Mo O'Hara**    **Jess Bradley**

D1419955

SCH

To my brother Matt, who introduced me
to comics and graphic novels and is my hero.
—M. O.

For Emma, without whom my childhood
would have been far duller (but also
with far less NKOTB). Miss you.
—J. B.

Published in the UK by Scholastic, 2022
Euston House, 24 Eversholt Street, London, NW1 1DB
Scholastic Ireland, 89E Lagan Road, Dublin Industrial Estate,
Glasnevin, Dublin, D11 HP5F

SCHOLASTIC and associated logos are trademarks and/or
registered trademarks of Scholastic Inc.

First published in the US by Macmillan Publishing Group, 2021

Text © Mo O'Hara, 2021
Illustrations © Jess Bradley, 2021
This edition published by arrangement with Feiwel and Friends, an imprint of Macmillan Publishing
Group LLC. All rights reserved.

The right of Mo O'Hara and Jess Bradley to be identified
as the author and illustrator of this work has been asserted by them under the Copyright,
Designs and Patents Act 1988.

ISBN 978 0702 31442 1

A CIP catalogue record for this book is available from the British Library.

Printed by C&C, China
Paper made from wood grown in sustainable forests and other controlled sources.

1 3 5 7 9 10 8 6 4 2

This is a work of fiction. Names, characters, places, incidents and dialogues are products
of the author's imagination or are used fictitiously. Any resemblance to actual people, living
or dead, events or locales is entirely coincidental.

www.scholastic.co.uk

Book design by Liz Dresner
Color by Jonh-Paul Bove
Lettering by Micah Myers

**Special Agent Anonymoose Personnel File**

**Size:** Extremely large

**Distinguishing features:** Antlers, dark brown hide, small birthmark that looks a little like North Dakota

**Talents:** Master of disguise, spying, investigating the strange (and possibly strange) goings-on in Woodland Territories, world-renowned Twister player

**Favorite item of clothing:** Snazzy investigating suit with lots of important pockets for spy stuff

**Clearance for spying:** First Class Spy Clearance for secrets

**Clearance for height:** About seven and a half feet

# Not-Quite-So-Special Agent Owlfred Personnel File

**Size:** Small enough that he can fit in a moose's pocket

**Distinguishing features:** Gray, feathery, can do that crazy owl thing where they twist their head most of the way around (but it makes him slightly motion sick)

**Talents:** Very precise analysis of clues and data, calm attitude in a crisis, patience in a crisis (also very good at just avoiding crises)

**Favorite item of clothing:** Exceedingly tiny bowler hat that he's been told accentuates his fetching feathery ears

**Clearance for spying:** Third Class Spy Clearance for secrets

**Clearance for height:** Irrelevant due to flying and all

Anonymoose, I know things are a bit slow at the moment, but...why is there a barbershop quartet of magpies singing about you?

Don't you just love the magpies' song, Owlfred? I thought I needed a theme tune, so I hired them. You remember them from the Case of the Missing Shiny Things?

Yes, case 87.

Flip!

Found!

Besides, I've decided that an agent without a theme tune is like a moose without antlers.

Like an owl without a hoot.

Like a magpie without a shiny thing. Oh, by the way, here's your sparkly calculator back.

Thanks...

It's like a newspaper Newt without a story.

Ahhhh!

Hi there. I thought I would stop by to see what's going on at Woodland HQ. Any stories brewing?

No stories brewing—just hot cocoa.

Yes, please, Owlfred. Seven sugars. I can't stop for stories now, Newt. I have family coming to visit and a theme tune to listen to. I'm a very busy moose, you know.

Oh, and here's your shiny watch back, Anonymoose.

How did you...? Never mind...

Jumping jackrabbits, I'm late! I need to get to the train station.

Chapter 2

Hup!

Train Station

THE MAGNIFICENT
MOOSEINI

# The Magnificent Mooseini

# AGENT MOOSE

Yes, it was always a surprise party when Granny Moose came to my birthdays.

⬇Flashback!⬇

Yay!

BOOM!

SPLAT!

Granny Moose! How was your trip? We thought you were coming by train.

No, I just thought the station would be a nice open place for me to drop in. How are you, my little Moosey Goosey? Give your Granny Moose a hug.

Oh, you'd never get Anonymoose up there. I remember we tried to get you on the trapeze one time when you visited the circus, and you just hung there with your eyes closed saying "Pleeeeeeease get me down. I'm tall enough when I'm on the ground."

Are you scared of heights, Anonymoose?

I just have a healthy respect for anything taller than my antlers.

Granny Moose is a circus stunt moose. She does all kinds of tricks and stunts.

But I'm retiring now. The circus is in town and my last performance is tonight.

Hang on...you're the Magnificent Mooseini!!! I've seen you on the posters!

MAGNIFICENT

MOOSEINI!!

Oh, are they still using that old picture? Gosh. I just wanted some family time with my grandson. I didn't know you would bring all these friends to meet me, Nony. Who's this dashing anteater, then?

I don't actually know any anteaters, Granny.

WAVE!

Agent Moose. We're sorry to intrude on family time, but there is an urgent mission that needs your attention. Animals in the forest are terrified. They are being intimidated into giving up their prize possessions by someone, but they are too afraid to say who is scaring them. You need to find out who is putting the squeeze on these forest animals and put a stop to it. This could be a dangerous character, Anonymoose, so use utmost caution.

This message will be sucked up by an anteater in one second.

Slup!

Wait. What happened to the chipmunk who used to suck up all the urgent messages? She was a very good agent, if a bit wiffy.

Yes, she still is. A good agent, I mean. But a bit less wiffy now that she discovered she is digitally intolerant.

Digitally intolerant?

If there's a ride, I wouldn't mind coming too.

There is no ride!

Just difficult investigating.

And serious analyzing.

That doesn't sound nearly as fun as a ride.

Well, I still want to come along and see my Nony investigate something.

Granny, we can't take you along on official Woodland HQ business. What if you got hurt?

Anony, honey, I've been in more dangerous situations than you've rubbed fuzz off your antlers.

Ah, antler fuzz.

Non-moose → Huh?!

It's a moose thing.

All right, you can come along, Granny, but just to observe.

Wooo eeeeey!

I'm just a bit excited. And I can't hold in a good old moose bellow when I'm excited.

# AGENT MOOSE

# AGENT MOOSE

By using a time-honored crime-solving technique that sleuths have used for decades...

And what's that?

We're going to blend in with the witnesses so they'll relax and, hopefully, reveal the robber. Then we'll meet you and Newt at the cocoa shop. And I think I know just where to start!

knows what's coming!

Chapter 5

Cocoa Shop

At least the bears fell asleep when the magpies started that lullaby? Or you'd still be there.

NEW!

Cocoa FRAPP!

Please order ☆ here! ↓

But we don't know anything else about whoever is putting the squeeze on animals.

Snacks!

MISSION MAYHEM

Several Tupperware containers of food.

A crate of coconuts.

A pirate hat.

A feather boa.

Oh, and a deed to a time-share property in the Hamptons.

What can we say? We find a lot of stuff.

49

Remember how I always got you to eat your greens even when you didn't want to?

I still don't like greens, but yes...you made it into a game.

✿Wink!✿

Follow my lead.

# AGENT MOOSE

# Mission Mayhem

And I can go to the Woodland HQ data archive and see what I can find out about a snake who puts the squeeze on people. Maybe they have a record?

So, Anonymoose... you know what would be a fun game?

Filing!! Yaaay! Fun with Filing! Doesn't that sound like a great game, Anonymoose?

It only works when Granny does it, Owlfred.

Oh. Never mind, then.

While you're out doing your research, I can show Granny around the Big Woods and see if we spot anything out of the ordinary or ask if anyone has seen a snake. I'm a moose on a mission.

We're both moose on a mission. Woooo eeey!

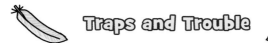

# Traps and Trouble

It's funny, there's no one around. Everyone in the Big Woods must be scared. We have to find this snake and find it fast!

I feel like I'm taking you away from your investigating, Nony.

Unless we get a lead on the identity of the robber from Owlfred's data analysis, this investigation has hit a brick wall.

I really wish it was an actual wall. That would be so much easier.

We can smash through this, though. There's got to be a way to find this snake. I'm just not seeing it.

Trip!

Sproing!

# Traps and Trouble

# Traps and Trouble

## Name:
Anna-CON-da

## Description:
Colorful 15-ft snake
with lots of muscle

## Whereabouts:
Recently released
from Woodland Prison.
Whereabouts unknown

## Hobbies:
Accordion playing. Making fresh-
squeezed orange juice

## Criminal Convictions:
Robbery, intimidation of forest animals

## MO (Most Obvious way
of doing crimes):
Putting the squeeze on folks and
forcing them to give away their
possessions

# The Big Squeeze

# AGENT MOOSE

# The Big Squeeze

# The Big Squeeze

# The Big Squeeze

# Treasure Hunt

# Treasure Hunt

# AGENT MOOSE

Actually, I think you'll find that you're under arrest. Or about to be under arrest. I would arrest you myself if I wasn't completely trapped in your coils.

It's kinda tight, honey. Do you think you can loosen up a bit?

Right, sorry, wait. So, if you're not going to arrest me, then who is?

# Treasure Hunt

# Snakes and Ladders

Okay, enough about what's good for you. You're gonna tell me where I can get the loot and then you're gonna stay quiet until I'm gone. You got it?

Nod!

Angry point!

Actually, there isn't any loot. We just said that to lure you here so we could arrest you for putting the squeeze on folks in the forest.

No loot? So you've been wasting my time? Now what should I do with you both?

# Snakes and Ladders

Swing!

We knew you could do it, Anonymoose.

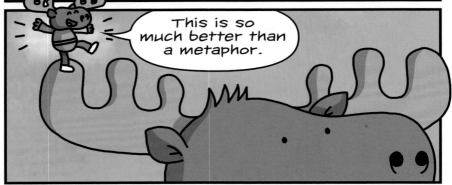

# High Stakes High Wire

Chapter 11

LAIRS AND LOOT

# Lairs and Loot

You have really nice stuff, but it was wrong of me to take it. And wrong of me to put the squeeze on you to stay quiet about it. If I get anxious, I just can't help squeezing. I was so scared that if anyone knew I was stealing I would have to go back to jail.

Well, at least you recognize that you were wrong.

You scared a lot of animals though, Anna-con-da.

Sometimes I don't know my own strength. I promise I won't put the squeeze on any more animals. I'm sorry I scared everyone. What can I do to make it up to everyone?

Well, you could put your squeezing to good use.

Yes, instead of going back to prison, maybe you could help out here.

# Lairs and Loot

Thanks, animals. I won't scare anyone anymore and when I'm done helping everyone that needs it, I'll head out of the Big Woods and won't cause any more trouble for any of you.

Actually, I might have another idea of what you can do.

Backstage

That was amazing. And we get to do that every day? As a job?

Sure. When you're not helping out the other animals.

You're a natural stunt snake. I spotted your potential the first time you coiled us up to the trapeze platform.

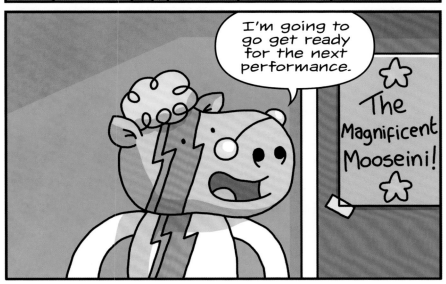

My little Nony! Now I can retire happy— once I've trained Anna-con-da to be the best darn stunt snake in the business, of course. Anytime you want to join me on the tightrope, Nony, just let me know.

Hug!

I think I'm fine on the ground really. In the future I'll try and leave the flying to Owlfred.

That's good. I don't fancy any more jumping jackrabbits for a while.

Or right above me, maybe? The bears said they would give us a lift back on the scenic route along the tracks. Fancy a ride home?

**Geronimoooooooooooooooose!!!**

Ahem... **Woooo eeey!**

THANK YOU FOR READING

The Friends who made

possible are:

Jean Feiwel, Publisher

Liz Szabla, Associate Publisher

Rich Deas, Senior Creative Director

Holly West, Senior Editor

Anna Roberto, Senior Editor

Kat Brzozowski, Senior Editor

Dawn Ryan, Senior Managing Editor

Erin Siu, Associate Editor

Rachel Diebel, Assistant Editor

Emily Settle, Associate Editor

Foyinsi Adegbonmire, Editorial Assistant

Kim Waymer, Senior Production Manager

Liz Dresner, Associate Art Director

Mandy Veloso, Senior Production Editor